APPETIZERS

KOOKY COOKERY

AN ARCHIVE OF IRREGULAR RECIPES FROM YESTERYEAR

BY BRYAN BALLINGER

APPLEWOOD BOOKS
Carlisle, Massachusetts

WIN WITH FOOD

Food management, one of wartime's most important jobs, rests squarely on the shoulders of the American homemaker. Food will win the war and make the peace only if it is administered wisely by the meal planners of the nation, so that supplies will be adequate to meet the ever-increasing demands.

Knowing about food is more essential today than ever before in history. In times like these it is not enough to have a few pet recipes. You have to broaden your food knowledge and honestly look beyond personal tastes and life-time habits, in order to be able to view the food picture as a whole.

You should resolve to get out of that old food rut so that you are ready to meet big shifts in shortages and supplies. You should try to conserve in every way possible. Above all you must choose foods that will provide maximum nourishment, and learn how to prepare them correctly, so as to avoid loss of nutrients through improper cooking. In these ways you will help to assure for your family the energy and good health needed to handle added tasks and stepped-up activities. Here is your chance, too—as a homemaker—to contribute directly to winning the war.

These Cook Books have been prepared to help you not only through present days of readjustment but in happier times to follow—when the lessons in nutrition, thrift and adaptability now being learned will make better food managers of us all.

IN THE 1940S, MANY AMERICAN WOMEN ENTERED THE WORKFORCE TO REPLACE THE MEN GOING OFF TO WAR. LATER, THESE WOMEN NEEDED TO BE TRANSITIONED BACK INTO THE HOME TO MAKE ROOM FOR THE RETURNING SOLDIERS. WHAT BETTER WAY TO FACILITATE THIS EXODUS THAN WITH RECIPE BOOKLETS THAT GLAMORIZED THE HOMEMAKER? HENCE, MANY OF THE RECIPES IN THIS BOOK!

TABLE OF CONTENTS

Appetizers

Salads

Chilled peeled tomatoes filled with goose livers in jelly and served with tiny sandwiches are for the hostess who seeks new ideas.
DURING YOUR CULINARY JOURNEY THROUGH YESTER-YEAR, BE SURE TO TAKE NOTICE OF THE PINNED-UP QUOTES! THESE ARE FROM THE ORIGINAL RECIPE SOURCES!

APPETIZERS

FIRST UP, WE HAVE SOME VINTAGE BLACK-AND-WHITE RECIPES FROM THE EARLY ARCHIVES. ENJOY!
THE PERFECT WAY TO SET THE TONE FOR YOUR WHOLE EVENING: A TOOTHPICK AND A SQUARE OF SOMETHING UNIDENTIFIABLE.

BARBECUBES

INGREDIENTS

1 package (3 ounces) jello lemon, orange, or orange-pineapple gelatin

1 cup boiling water

1 can (8 ounces) tomato sauce

1 1/2 tablespoons vinegar

1/2 teaspoon salt

Dash pepper

DIRECTIONS

Dissolve gelatin in boiling water.

Add remaining ingredients.

Pour into 8-inch square pan; chill until firm.

Cut into cubes and serve on salad greens.

Makes about 2 cups, 4 side salads, or 6 relish servings.

CARBUNCLE BALLS

INGREDIENTS

2 egg whites

1 cup grated American cheese

Dash cayenne

1/4 cup grated dry bread crumbs

DIRECTIONS

Beat egg whites until stiff.

Add cheese, cayenne, and bread crumbs.

Pat into small balls and fry in hot deep fat (375°F) until light brown.

Makes about 16 balls.

Crispy, browned cheese ball appetizers are a happy surprise to almost everyone.

CHEESE 'N' RICE OOZER ORBS

RICE INGREDIENTS

4 cups cooked rice

Salt and pepper to taste

Dash paprika

4 teaspoons onion juice

8 tablespoons butter or margarine, melted

6 tomato slices

CHEESE SAUCE INGREDIENTS

3/4 pound American cheese, grated

3/4 cup milk

RICE DIRECTIONS

Season rice with salt, pepper, paprika, the onion juice, and butter or margarine.

Pack into 6 well-greased custard cups and place in a pan of water in an oven at 250°F for a few minutes, until heated through.

Turn each rice mold out on a large tomato slice and top with cheese sauce.

CHEESE SAUCE DIRECTIONS

Melt the cheese in the top of a double boiler; add the milk gradually and blend until smooth.

Cook until sauce has thickened.

Serve over rice molds on tomato slices.

PAN-GALACTIC PARTY PLATTER

INGREDIENTS

1 head cabbage

Sour cream dressing

8 gherkins

8 cocktail frankfurters

8 pearl onions

8 olives

8 cheese cubes

DIRECTIONS

Wash cabbage and remove outside leaves. Cut a slice from top and remove center, leaving a shell. Shred cabbage from center, mix thoroughly with cream dressing, and chill. When ready to serve, fill center with shredded cabbage. Spear remaining ingredients on hors d'oeuvres picks and stick picks outside of cabbage head, alternating. Surround with butter crackers or other hors d'oeuvres. Alternatively, fill center with chicken, shrimp, or crab-meat salad, saving center cabbage to be served creamed or fried.

CRISP KRINGLES

FESTIVE AND SUGGESTIVE BANANA CANDLES

INGREDIENTS

1 1/2 envelopes (1 1/2 tablespoons) unflavored gelatin

1/3 cup cold water

2 cups canned cranberry juice cocktail

4 ripe bananas

8 salted almonds

Mayonnaise

Salad greens

DIRECTIONS

Soften gelatin in cold water.

Heat cranberry cocktail to boiling; add to gelatin and stir into dissolved gelatin.

Pour into 8 small, star-shaped molds. Chill until firm. Unmold.

Cut out and remove a small circle from the center of each star the same diameter as the bananas.

Peel bananas; cut in halves, crosswise. Insert 1/2 banana in the center of each star as shown.

Top each "candle" with a salted almond for a "flame." Add a little mayonnaise to look like melted wax.

Serve on salad greens with mayonnaise. Makes 8 servings.

FESTIVE AND SUGGESTIVE BANANA CANDLES

DON'T FORGET TO BLOW OUT THE NUT-WICKS BEFORE YOU EAT THESE "CANDLES."

SALADS

THE TIME HAS COME FOR A RETURN TO THE VALUES OF YESTERYEAR, OR AT LEAST A RETURN TO A BROADER DEFINITION OF THE TERM "SALAD." WHO NEEDS FRESH FRUIT AND VEGETABLES ANYWAY?

GLEAMING TOMATO INGOT

INGREDIENTS

1 envelope Knox Unflavored Gelatin

1 3/4 cups tomato juice, divided

1/4 teaspoon salt

1/2 teaspoon sugar

1/2 teaspoon Worcestershire sauce

1/8 teaspoon Tabasco

2 tablespoons lemon juice

DIRECTIONS

Sprinkle gelatin on 1/2 cup of the tomato juice to soften.

Place over low heat and stir until gelatin is dissolved.

Remove from heat and stir in remaining 1 1/4 cups tomato juice and seasonings.

Turn into a 2-cup mold or individual molds.

Chill until firm.

Unmold on serving plate. Garnish with salad greens, cucumber slices, and black olives. Serve with salad dressing.

Sparkling and refreshing Tomato Aspic adds a bright touch to any meal with its shimmering goodness.

JELLIED LAWN CLUMP

INGREDIENTS

1 envelope Knox
    Unflavored Gelatin

1 tablespoon sugar

1 teaspoon salt

1/8 teaspoon pepper

1 3/4 cups water, divided

1/4 cup vinegar

1 tablespoon lemon juice

1/4 cup chopped scallions

1 cup shredded raw
    spinach

1 cup chopped celery

1/4 cup shredded raw
    carrots

DIRECTIONS

Mix gelatin, sugar, salt, and
    pepper in a saucepan. Add
    1/2 cup of the water.

Place over low heat, stirring
    constantly until gelatin is
    dissolved.

Remove from heat and stir in
    remaining 1 1/4 cups water,
    vinegar, and lemon juice.

Chill mixture to unbeaten egg
    white consistency. Fold in
    scallions, spinach, celery,
    and carrots.

Turn into 3-cup mold or
    individual molds and chill
    until firm.

Unmold by dipping mold in
    warm water to depth of the
    gelatin. Loosen around
    edge with tip of a paring
    knife.

Place serving dish on top of
    mold; turn upside down.
    Shake, holding disk tightly
    to mold. Garnish with
    tomatoes and olives.

JELLIED LAWN CLUMP

A new and deliciously different twist for a popular stand-by – green salad is molded for added pleasure.

VEGETABLE AND VINEGAR JIGGLERS

INGREDIENTS

1 envelope Knox Gelatin

1/4 cup cold water

1 cup hot water

1/4 cup mild vinegar

1 tablespoon lemon juice

1/2 teaspoon salt

1 1/2 cups diced or shredded vegetables (raw or cooked)

1-2 tablespoons sugar (or more to taste)

Dash pepper

1 tablespoon finely minced onion, if desired

DIRECTIONS

Soften gelatin in cold water and dissolve in hot water.

Add vinegar, lemon juice, salt, sugar, and pepper. Cool.

When mixture begins to thicken, fold in vegetables.

Turn into 6 individual molds that have been rinsed in cold water, and chill.

When firm, unmold on salad greens and serve with desired dressing.

VEGETABLE AND VINEGAR JIGGLERS

IF YOUR
SALAD STARTS JIGGLING
ON ITS OWN, STAY CLEAR OF EXTERIOR
WALLS, GET UNDER A TABLE,
AND HOLD ON.

FIRMLY GIRDLED GAZPACHO

INGREDIENTS

2 envelopes unflavored
  gelatin
1 can (1.2 ounces) tomato
  juice
1/3 cup red wine vinegar
1 teaspoon salt
Tabasco
2 small tomatoes, peeled
  and diced (1 cup)
1 medium cucumber, pared
  and diced
1/2 medium green pepper,
  diced
1/4 cup finely chopped red
  onion
1 tablespoon chopped
  chives
2 large ripe avocados
Lemon juice
1/3 cup bottled oil-and-
  vinegar dressing
Watercress

DIRECTIONS

In medium saucepan, sprinkle gelatin over 3/4 cup tomato juice to soften. Place over low heat, stirring constantly, until gelatin is dissolved. Remove from heat.

Stir in remaining tomato juice, vinegar, salt, and several drops Tabasco. Set in bowl of ice, stirring occasionally, until mixture is consistency of unbeaten egg white (about 15 minutes).

Fold in tomato, cucumber, green pepper, onion, and chives until well combined. Pour into fluted, 1 1/2-quart mold that has been rinsed in cold water. Refrigerate until firm (at least 6 hours).

To unmold: Run small spatula around edge of mold; invert over serving platter; place a hot, damp dishcloth over inverted mold, and shake gently to release. Refrigerate.

Just before serving, peel and slice avocados. Brush with lemon juice. Arrange avocado slices around molded salad, and pour dressing over them. Garnish with watercress.

I STAB AT THEE AND THY HEART OF CELERY

(WITH WATERCRESS AND ANCHOVIES)

INGREDIENTS

3 medium celery hearts

1 medium onion, sliced

1 can (10 1/2 ounces) condensed beef broth, undiluted

1 bottle (8 ounces) French dressing

Watercress sprigs or chopped spinach

1 tomato, cut in 6 wedges

1 red pepper, cut in 6 rings

1 can (2 ounces) rolled anchovy fillets with capers, drained

1 can (4 ounces) pitted ripe olives, drained

DIRECTIONS

Wash celery; trim root ends. Discard all but the smallest leaves.

In medium skillet, combine celery hearts, onion, beef broth, and 1 1/4 cups water. Bring to a boil; reduce heat and simmer, covered, 15 minutes, or until celery is tender.

Remove from heat. Let celery stand in broth to cool.

Drain celery. Cut each heart in half lengthwise. Arrange in shallow dish. Pour French dressing over celery. Refrigerate several hours, or until very cold.

To serve: Arrange watercress sprigs or chopped spinach on each of 6 chilled salad plates. With slotted spoon, place half a celery heart on greens on each plate. Garnish each with 1 tomato wedge, 1 pepper ring, a few anchovy fillets, and olives. Pass dressing remaining from celery marinade.

SHREDDED VEGETABLE
SUSPENSION

INGREDIENTS

2 envelopes unflavored
  gelatin

1/2 cup sugar

1 teaspoon salt

1 can (12 ounces) apple juice

1/2 cup lemon juice

2 tablespoons vinegar

1 cup shredded carrot

1 cup sliced celery

1 cup finely shredded
  cabbage

1/2 cup chopped green
  pepper

1 can (4 ounces)
  chopped pimiento

DIRECTIONS

In small saucepan, combine
  gelatin, sugar, and salt; mix
  well. Add 1 cup water. Stir
  constantly over low heat
  until sugar and gelatin are
  dissolved. Remove from
  heat.

Stir in apple juice, lemon juice,
  vinegar, and 1/4 cup cold
  water. Pour into medium
  bowl. Refrigerate 1 hour, or
  until mixture is consistency
  of unbeaten egg white.

Add carrot, celery, cabbage,
  green pepper, and pimiento;
  stir until well combined.

Turn into decorative, 1 1/2-
  quart mold. Refrigerate 4
  hours, or until firm.

To unmold: Run small spatula
  around edge of mold; invert
  onto serving plate. Place
  hot dishcloth over mold;
  shake gently to release.
  Repeat, if necessary. Lift
  off mold. Refrigerate until
  ready to serve.

Written, compiled, designed, and photographed
by Bryan Ballinger
Visit Bryan at www.breadwig.com

This book is dedicated to Susan Goodman.

Character model: Jennifer Ballinger
Graphics production: Merrill Ballinger

Also available in the Kooky Cookery series:
BRUNCH, JELLO, and MEAT!

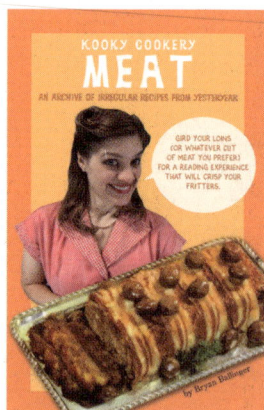

To inquire about this edition or to request a free copy
of our current catalog featuring our best-selling books, write to:
Applewood Books
P.O. Box 27
Carlisle, MA 01741
For more complete listings, visit us on the web at: www.awb.com

10 9 8 7 6 5 4 3 2 1

MANUFACTURED IN THE UNITED STATES OF AMERICA